That Potato Ain't That Big

Darrell W. Henry

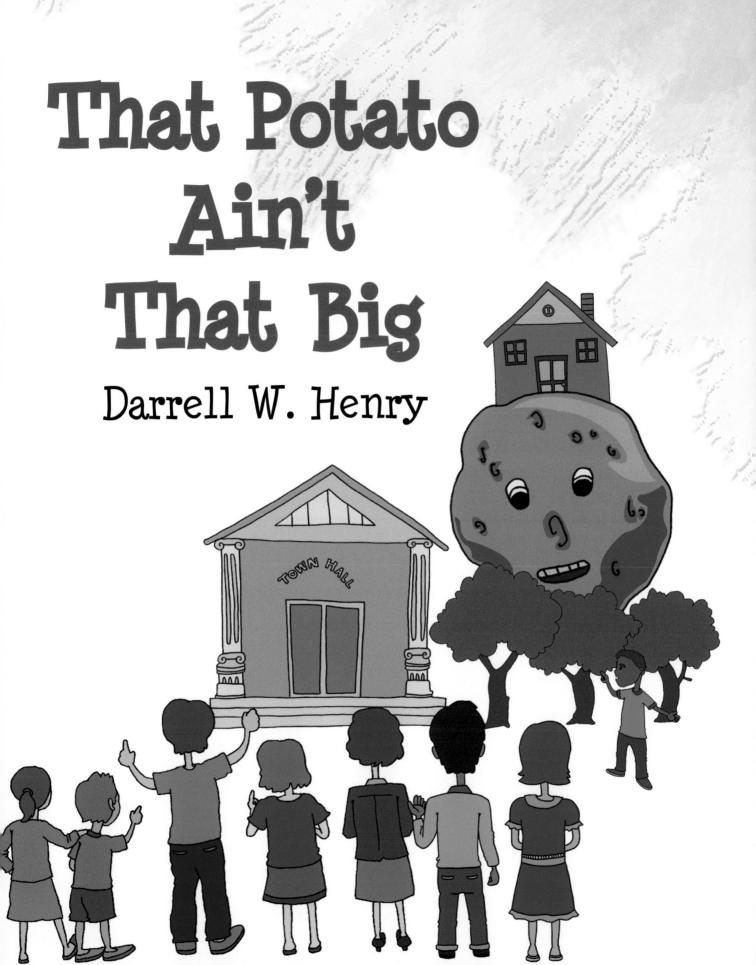

To order additional copies of this book, contact:
Xlibris
1-888-795-4274
www.Xlibris.com
Orders@Xlibris.com

ISBN: Softcover 978-1-4415-8140-2
Hardcover 978-1-4415-8141-9
EBook 978-1-9845-8735-0

Library of Congress Control Number: 2009909733

Print information available on the last page

Rev. date: 06/29/2020

This book is dedicated
to my Grandparents
William and Cleo Henry.
They taught me to love who I am
and to take care of my family.

While reading to the kids, point to them and let them say "That potato ain't that big!" everytime it shows up in the book. Try to substitute the kid's name in the book with the name of the kid you are reading to.

Once upon a time in a little town called Spudsville, there lived a little boy named D.J. His family was poor and got by on very little, but they were always happy.

D.J. had lots of friends and would get into many arguments because he did not always tell the truth, and he did not always listen to others.

One day when D.J. was playing
in his backyard he tripped over
a large root. "Ouch" he cried out.
"Where is this root coming from?"

So, he followed the root all the way across the backyard and into his basement. To his surprise a giant potato the size of the moon was there.

"Wow" D.J. yelled.
Just as he started
to run to tell his
parents, the potato
said "Hello D.J.
How are you?"

HELLO

In amazement D.J.
stopped in his tracks
and turned around.
"Wow" he said.
He walked slowly
toward the giant potato.
"Am I dreaming,
or did you just talk?"

"Yes, said the giant potato.
My name is Khalil,
and I am a magic potato.

"Wow" said D.J. If you're magic,
I wish for a new bike, and a new house,
and a million dollars."

"Hold on!" said Khalil.
"My magic will only work
when the time is right.
You must not tell anyone
about me.

"Oh, I won't tell anyone"
D.J. said as he turned to
leave his basement.

Now as soon as D.J left the basement he ran to tell his parents. "There's a potato in the basement as big as the moon".

His parents said "D.J., **that potato ain't that big!** Now go outside and play with your friends and stop making up things like that."

D.J. put his head down and walked outside to play.

His friend Adrian was riding his scooter.
D.J. ran over to Adrian and began telling
the same story of the giant potato.

Adrian looked at D.J. and said, **"That potato ain't that big!"**

"Well it is that big" D.J. said as he stormed off
to play with someone else who would believe him.

He went to the park where two of his good friends,
Mia and Dominique, were playing hopscotch. When D.J.
saw them he ran to them saying "hey you guys,
I have something really, really important to tell you.
You have to believe me."

"OK, OK, tell us already" said Mia.

"Well, I have a potato as big as the moon in my basement
and he can talk."

Mia and Dominique looked at each other and started to
laugh as they both said **"That potato ain't that big."**

"But it is, I tell ya, it is."

D.J. ran off. He was very upset. "Someone has got to believe me" he said to himself.

So D.J. decided to go to the mayor of Spudsville, Mrs. Washington.

Here in Spudsville, potatoes are a big deal. They are a part of life for the people of Spudsville. They are used to make potato clothes, potato shoes, potato hats, potato houses, and the people even drive potato cars. Without potatoes the town would disappear.

Now Mrs. Washington knows about D.J. and his way of not telling the truth. So when D.J. came running into her office, Ms. Washington knew she was in for a story.

D.J. said "In my basement I have the largest potato in the world. It is as big as the moon" he said as he stretched his arms to show her how big.

Mrs. Washington was very upset that D.J. would say a thing like that and she didn't believe him. But if it were true that would make D.J. the richest man in Spudsville.

She looked at D.J.
and said with a stern voice
"That potato ain't that big!"

That made D.J. very sad and angry.
So angry that he wanted to run away
because no one would believe him.
But because he was a little boy,
he couldn't run away too far. He had
no food or potato money to live on.

So he just hid in the back
of his house in an old red
wooden tree house.

He stayed in the tree house for a long, long time, and then he fell asleep. While sleep he was awakened by a loud windy sound, **"swish, swish."**

D.J. jumped out of the tree house and ran to see if he could tell where the sound was coming from.

As he approached the front yard
he noticed all his neighbors
on their knees crying,
"waaaahhh, waaaahhh."

"What's wrong?" yelled D.J.

One of his friends Aaron said
that a swarm of killer potato
bugs came and grabbed all
the potatoes in Spudsville
and there are none left.

Waaaaahhhh, there is nothing left. What are we going to do? Without potatoes we can't survive. We are all going to disappearrrrrrr said Aaron.

Now D.J. just knew he had to do something about saving the town. So he went to his basement and told Khalil the magic potato everything that was going on.

Khalil said "OK, I have a plan. But you have to follow it completely, or it will not work. If you do not follow it completely I will be gone and the town will disappear as well. Go and let the people know..

D.J. knew that this might be
a big task for a little boy and that no one
would believe him. He did not let that stop him.

He jumped on his scooter and scooted across town
and gathered all the people of Spudsville in front
of the potato town hall.

"People of Spudsville, as you know all of our potatoes are gone. But I have a solution to our problem."

"What is it?" the people asked.

"Well," he said, "In my basement I have a potato the size of the moon. It's magic. It will solve all our problems."

The people got angry at D.J. and they all yelled at once **"That potato ain't that big!"**

Suddenly, a loud crashing sound
came from behind the crowd.
The crowd turned around
and a giant potato the size
of the moon was growing
behind the trees.

It grew so big that people
had to lie on their backs
to see the top of it.
At the very top of the
giant potato was
D.J.'s house.

Then all the people of Spudsville shouted at once, "**That potato is that big**".

The huge potato winked and suddenly potatoes began growing everywhere. The people began clapping and shouting because once again they would be able to make all their potato things.

All at once the big potato disappeared.

The people of Spudsville turned around and looked at D.J.

They were so happy that all of them began to laugh and cry. They picked D.J. up, threw him in the air, then his father put him on his shoulder and carried him to the spot where their house once was.

The mayor gave D.J. the key to the city.

Then people of Spudsville built D.J.'s family the biggest house in the town, and they all lived happily ever after.

The Mayor gave Jill the key to the city.

Then people of Smallville told Jill about
the biggest house in the town, and they all
lived happily ever after.

Printed in the United States
By Bookmasters